Prehistoric Creatures Then and Now

TRICERATOPS

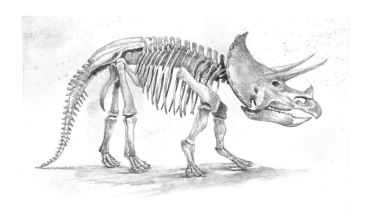

By Lara Bergen
Illustrated by
Steven James Petruccio

Steadwell Books

Raintree Steck-Vaughn Publishers
A Harcourt Company

Austin · New York
www.steck-vaughn.com

Special thanks to Paul Marsh, Paleontology Researcher,
American Museum of Natural History

Produced by By George Productions, Inc.

Published by Raintree Steck-Vaughn Publishers,
an imprint of Steck-Vaughn Company

Library of Congress Cataloging-in-Publication Data
Bergen, Lara.
    Triceratops / Lara Bergen
        p.   cm — (Prehistoric creatures then and now)
    Summary: Describes the characteristics and habits of the plant-
eating dinosaur, as well as theories about why it became extinct.
Includes index.
    ISBN 0-7398-0103-1
    1. Triceratops — Juvenile literature. [1. Triceratops.
2. Dinosaurs.]
    I. Title. II. Series.
    QE862.O65.B48   2000
    567.915'8 — dc21   99-055479

Printed and bound in the United States of America
10 9 8 7 6 5 4 3 2 1 LB 03 02 01 00

Photo Acknowledgments:
Pages 8, 22: Department of Library Services, American Museum of
Natural History; Page 24: Royal Tyrrell Museum of
Paleontology/Alberta Community Development; Page 26: © J. B.
Lafitte/Explorer, Photo Researchers, Inc.

Contents

"Three-Horned Face"

Imagine a creature as big as a minivan. Its head is bigger than you are. On its head are three mean-looking horns. It is huge and strong. But it is gentle. It is called Triceratops. This means "three-horned face."

Triceratops lived some 65 million years ago. It lived in what we now call North America. But back then North America was very different. A sea ran down the middle of North America, from Canada to the Gulf of Mexico.

Triceratops's horns were a main feature.

 4

Triceratops lived on the sea's warm coasts.

Like all other dinosaurs, Triceratops was an early reptile. It had thick skin. It walked on straight legs. It lived on land and laid eggs. But there were many things that made Triceratops different, too.

Time Line

Mesozoic
(The era of the dinosaurs)

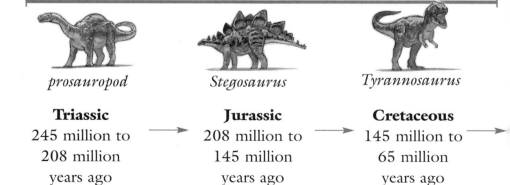

prosauropod	*Stegosaurus*	*Tyrannosaurus*
Triassic	**Jurassic**	**Cretaceous**
245 million to 208 million years ago	208 million to 145 million years ago	145 million to 65 million years ago

6

Triceratops roamed open plains looking for food.

Cenozoic
(The era of mammals, including humans)

mammoth

human

Tertiary
65 million to
5 million
years ago

Quaternary
1.6 million
years ago
to today

Horns

Triceratops belonged to a group of dinosaurs called ceratopsians—or "horned dinosaurs." It was one of the biggest of all the horned dinosaurs. Like all horned dinosaurs, Triceratops was a plant eater.

Triceratops had one short horn on its nose. And it had two longer horns above its eyes. Some horns were as tall as you are! What were these horns for?

A Triceratops model

Triceratops ate plants and parts of trees.

Some scientists think Triceratops used its horns to defend itself against meat eaters like Tyrannosaurus rex or Utah raptor. Triceratops probably did not run much. But it could run fast. It might have scared enemies away by charging at them with its horns—as rhinoceroses do today.

9

Other scientists think that Triceratops's horns were used mostly to help it get food. Triceratops could have used its horns to bend tall trees. In that way it could reach the tasty leaves at the top.

Triceratops also used its strong, birdlike beak to tear through woody pieces. Then it used its sharp teeth to chew up the plants. As old teeth wore down, new teeth grew in their place. Triceratops ate bushes, pine needles, and other plants that many other dinosaurs could not eat.

Triceratops probably also used its horns the way most horned animals use them today. Like horned deer and sheep, male Triceratops might have locked horns and had pushing contests. The winner might become the herd leader. Or it might win a mate.

Triceratops might have used its horns to bend tall trees in order to reach the leaves close to the top.

The Frill

Triceratops had a huge frill, or bony plate, that covered its neck. There are no animals today that have anything like it. What was it for?

Did it keep Triceratops's neck safe from mighty meat eaters like Tyrannosaurus rex? Maybe. The frill was very heavy and was covered with tough skin. Marks of Tyrannosaurus rex teeth have been found in Triceratops frill fossils.

The big, heavy frill probably also helped balance Triceratops's strong jaw muscles.

Some scientists believe the frill might even have helped Triceratops keep cool or warm.

 12

The frill bone was not solid. It had tiny channels, or paths, running through it. This makes scientists think that the frill was filled with many blood vessels. As the blood pumped through the frill, the air around would cool or warm the blood. Elephants' ears help keep them cool in much the same way.

Triceratops probably also used its frill the way it used its horns—to impress other members of its herd.

Triceratops's frill might have helped it cool off in water holes.

Triceratops and Its Young

How did Triceratops give birth to its young? Just as reptiles do today, Triceratops laid eggs. But most reptiles leave their eggs to open alone. The young must take care of themselves.

Scientists believe that Triceratops dug nests in sand and laid their eggs inside.

Unlike today's reptiles Triceratops probably did not leave their young alone.

Scientists believe that Triceratops lived in herds and that Triceratops mothers made nests in groups. They dug nests in the sand. Then they laid their eggs in them. The adults watched the eggs. When the babies hatched, the adults brought them food.

Fossils of adults and babies have been found near fossils of nests and eggs. This makes scientists think the babies stayed near the nests. They believe their parents cared for them until they were old enough to take care of themselves.

Triceratops may have lived in family groups.

Why Did Triceratops Disappear?

Triceratops was one of the last dinosaurs. When Triceratops roamed Earth, there were more kinds of dinosaurs than ever before. There were many different kinds of plants.

There were also mammals, other reptiles, birds, and fish. But then something happened. About 65 million years ago, the Cretaceous period ended, and the dinosaurs ended, too.

What happened? Most scientists think a huge rock—or maybe more than one rock—fell from space. It hit Earth and changed everything. The whole Earth would have shaken. Large waves would have flooded the land. Volcanoes might have erupted, changing the atmosphere. Forest fires would spread. Poisonous gas would have filled the air. The sun's light would have been blocked—maybe for years and years.

Some plants and animals would have died right away. Others would have died later because they had no clean water and nothing to eat. Big animals like Triceratops were not able to survive.

◀ Triceratops grazed for food until about 65 million years ago.

Most scientists think that a huge rock fell from space and caused the dinosaurs to die off.

Some scientists think the big rock—a meteorite—was not all that killed Triceratops. The earth's climate might also have been changing, making a difference in the seasons.

Right now we do not know exactly what happened. But scientists are always working to find out. Maybe one day they will find the answer. Maybe one day you will be the one to find the answer!

Othniel Marsh

 22

Dinosaur Namer

One day in 1887 a scientist named Othniel Marsh found three giant horn fossils on land near Denver, Colorado. Dr. Marsh was a paleontologist—a scientist who studies fossils. Fossils are the remains of ancient life.

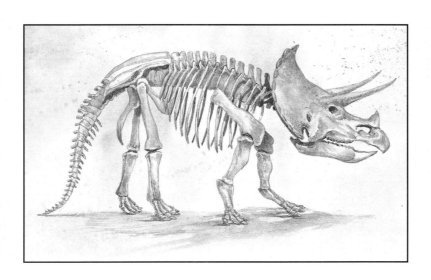

A Triceratops skeleton

At first Marsh thought he had found the horns of a huge prehistoric buffalo. Then a few months later Marsh's assistant, John Bell Hatcher, showed him a strange dinosaur skull he had found. Hatcher said it had "eyeholes as big as your hat" and three horns "as long as a hoe handle." The horns were just like the horns Marsh had found. That's when Marsh realized that the horns he had found were dinosaur horns, not buffalo horns. Dr. Marsh named this new dinosaur "Triceratops"—three-horned face—in honor of those horns.

Be a Dinosaur Detective

How do scientists know how dinosaurs like Triceratops lived? There are no photographs to look at. There are no true stories to read. There are only fossils—the remains of bones and teeth, horns and claws, eggs, and sometimes skin. But fossils can't tell you everything. They are only clues for dinosaur detectives. To imagine how Triceratops and other dinosaurs lived, scientists look at animals that are alive today.

◄ A Triceratops model

Because Triceratops had horns, scientists think it probably used them as horned animals do today. And they think Triceratops's frill was filled with blood vessels. It might have worked like an air conditioner, like the big ears of elephants.

To think like a dinosaur detective, look at Triceratops. Then look at big plant-eating animals alive now—like rhinoceroses and elephants. How do they get food? How do they protect themselves? The more you know about them, the more you may be able to guess about how Triceratops lived.

Dinosaur detectives dig for fossils.

Make a Triceratops Mask

Note: This is a little tricky, so ask a grown-up to help.

Materials:

- cone-shaped paper cups
- cardboard or oaktag
- two 12 in. (30.5 cm) pieces of string
- paints
- hole punch
- glue
- scissors

1. Cut the piece of cardboard into a shape like the pattern below. The shape should be about 11 in. (28 cm) square.

2. Paint eyes, nostrils, and a mouth on the cardboard to make a face. Punch holes for the eyes.

3. Use glue to attach three paper cones to the mask to make the horns. Two cones should go behind the eyes. The third cone should go between the nostrils, just above the mouth.

4. Punch a hole on each side of the mask. Thread one piece of string through each hole, and tie a knot behind your head. This will hold the mask in place.

Glossary

ceratopsian (sair-uh-TOP-see-an) The family of horned dinosaurs to which Triceratops belonged

Cretaceous period (kreh-TAY-shus) The last period of dinosaurs, between 145 million and 65 million years ago. This was the period in which Triceratops lived.

dinosaurs (DIE-nuh-sores) Land-dwelling reptiles that lived from 245 million to 65 million years ago

fossil (FAH-sill) Remains of ancient life, such as a dinosaur bone, footprint, or imprint in a rock

frill (FRIL) A bony outgrowth around an animal's neck

mammals (MAM-ulls) Warm-blooded animals, usually with hair, that feed their young with milk

meteorite (MEE-tee-uh-rite) A rocky object from space that strikes the earth's surface. It can be a few inches or several miles wide.

paleontologist (pay-lee-on-TAH-luh-jist) A scientist who studies fossils

prehistoric (PREE-his-tor-ik) Referring to time before written records

reptile (REP-tile) A group of air-breathing animals that lay eggs and usually have scaly skin

Triceratops (try-SAIR-uh-tops) A large plant-eating dinosaur that lived in North America during the Cretaceous period

Tyrannosaurus rex (tuh-ran-uh-SORE-us REX) A meat-eating dinosaur that lived in North America during the Cretaceous period

Utah raptor (YOU-tah RAP-tur) Found in Utah, a large member of a group of dinosaurs with a sharp, curved claw on each hand and foot

Index